For the Love of Ministry

Cheryl P. Rivers

ISBN-10: 0-615-5824-6-x
ISBN-13: 978-0-615-58246-7
Printed in the United States of America

Edited by Lynel Johnson Washington
504-237-1253
Lmaria23@hotmail.com

Cover Art Design by Najah B. Clemmons
Art entitled: "Praying Hands"

Dedication

To my loving, and supportive parents and brothers:
Samuel and Janice Rivers & Vincent and Devin Rivers

To my grandmother: Mrs. Virgie Vandross *I love you, Grandma!*

To my Apostle & First Lady:
Apostle Dr. Robert & Dr. Priscilla Vandross
I pray that this book gives you great encouragement!

To every believer, and every Ambassador of the Gospel:
I dedicate this book to you. Continue to do all that you do
for the love of ministry!

Acknowledgments
How Can I Say Thanks?

It's once again, Lord, that I give You praise and honor for allowing me to minister to Your people through my writing. Father, I owe *everything* to You. For You have given me a rare and precious gift, that will never be taken for granted.

How can I say thank you to the world's greatest family? Mommy, Daddy, I love you for your never-ending support, and all of your encouragement. May God bless you and keep you always and forever. To the best brothers any girl could ask for: Vince, Devin, I love you both very much. I pray God's richest blessings upon your lives. Always know (and remember) that you are blessed and highly favored of God!

Apostle Dr. Robert Vandross, and Dr. Priscilla Vandross, I am so honored, and so blessed to have the two of you a part of my family, and my life. I am truly thankful for the relationship that we have. The connection we share through our family, and spiritually so, means more to me than you'll ever know. I have grown so much in my walk with God, and have come to understand more about ministry through your leadership. I love you both dearly, and I thank you for your love, support, and encouragement.

To all of my relatives, friends, and church family: thank you so much for your love and support! I love you all very much.

Contents

Introduction

Ministry. Take a few moments to think about that word. What does it actually mean? What comes to mind when you think about it? Is it mega churches; the glitz and glamor of being in the spotlight? Perhaps it's singing in the choir on Sunday mornings, on the praise and worship team, or serving in the Missionary Society. Ministry means far more than being a part of a large church, and singing in the choir, or being a member of any other auxiliary. It's not about self-gratification, or being in the limelight. Those who labor faithfully in ministry are those who deny themselves for the sake of others. They make sacrifices that one normally would not have the courage to make. They are men and women who pour into the hearts and lives of others, when often times, they themselves are in need.

In these days and times, there is so much going on within the body of Christ. Nevertheless, we are now in a season where God is calling for ministries across this nation--all over the world-- to come back to Him, and set things in order that are out of order. He's calling for those who have His heart to step up to the plate, and stand up for what is right. And holiness is what is right. People of God, this is the mandate given to us by our heavenly Father. I encourage you, my sisters and brothers, to stand firm on the word of God. Keep your focus. Never lose sight of your true purpose; your destiny. Pray without ceasing; always meditating on the things of God. Remember, only what we do for Jesus Christ will last.

Your Keeper for Life

Stand my child,
In the midst of your circumstances.
Stand in the midst of the storms of life.
Kneel before Me; seek Me while I may be found.

I'm not far away; just only one prayer.
No one knows you like I do.
No one loves you like I do.
I'm here to take away your every care;
Your every fear.

I'm yours and you are Mine;
Nothing and no one will come between us.
Surely, I am able to carry you through every situation.
I am your keeper, and your sustainer;
Your giver of life.

Chosen to Worship

How I long to be in Your presence, oh God.
To commune and fellowship with the One true God;
My Savior and friend.

Being with You makes me forget all of my troubles,
All of my hurts, and failures.
It is from You that I receive joy.
It is from You, God, that I receive true happiness and love.

How beautiful it is to be a chosen vessel;
One to be used by You.
One chosen to fellowship with You in Your holy temple;
That perfect place of praise.

You look past my failures and short comings,
And You see a heart filled with so much love and adoration for You.
You see a heart that's fit for worship.

Keep me anchored in You, God.
Keep me grounded in Your word.
Hold me as I hold on to You with all my might.

I never want to fall too far from Your reach.
That's why I need You to guide me.
Be my guiding light each and everyday.

Thank You for choosing me to be in Your presence;
To fellowship with You in Your holy temple.
Thank You for making my heart fit for worship.
I love and adore You always.

You're Never Alone

I will be with you in the midst of your circumstance.
No matter the test and trial, I will be with you.
Circumstances and trials come on every hand,
But My love is with you.
My loving arms will shield you.
Deny not My glory.
Deny not My loving kindness towards you.
Stand firm on the promises I've made to you;
That I will provide for you;
That I will never leave nor forsake you.

Praise Him Still

(Written in memory of my beloved grandfather, Thomas A. Vandross, Sr.)

Since he went away, a strong void
Has been attached to my spirit man.
But yet, in the midst of my despair,
I must praise Him still.

Keeping a constant praise in my mouth,
A song in my spirit lightens the burdens.
It lifts the heaviness that I feel.

God, my Father, is my sustainer in troubled times.
He's my rock and my fortress.
Under His wings, I can hide, and find shelter.

Be Encouraged

I have the power to change any situation
Anyone who exalts himself, I have the power to bring down.
Those things that seem impossible to reach,
I have the power to make them possible.

All power is in My hands.
I am the Almighty God, and I change not.
Don't lose heart in difficult situations.
Don't faint in troubled times.
Stand firm on My word,
That I'll never leave you, nor will I forsake you.

Stand in the midst of your circumstances;
Those things that try to consume you.
In the midst of every trial, you must praise Me.

No matter what you go through, praise Me still.
Even in your shortcomings, praise Me.
When you feel less than the average man,
Know that My grace is upon you.

My love for you is greater than the greatest mountain;
Deeper than the deepest sea.
Be confident in this one thing;
That I am with you, My child.
My hand is upon your life.

I Am Your Everything

I am your shelter from the storms of life.
I am your strength in times of weakness.
I am your joy in times of sadness;
I am your hope in times of distress.

In your time of need, I am your provider.
Rest assured in knowing, My child,
That I, the Lord God, am your everything!

The Refiner's Fire

The Refiner's Fire;
A place of renewal,
A place of restoration and deliverance,
A place where God can make me over
Again in His likeness.

Refine and renew my heart,
My soul; my very being.
Create in me a clean heart.
Renew a right spirit in me.

Purify me through and through,
With the fire of Your love.
Breathe upon me with a fresh wind,
A fresh anointing.

Keep Pressing On

So many struggles, obstacles and trials;
Being tossed to and fro by battle after battle.
But through it all, in the midst of it all,
I hear You say, "Stand on My word."
He sees, hears, and knows all things.
He's right there for you; right there by your side.

Don't fret because of the actions of man.
Don't lose heart because of what they do.
Trust in Me, and know that it's all for the good.
It comes for the good of them that love Me.
Go forth in My name, and stand strong.
Stand through the storm, and know that I am with you always.

It's Time for War-ship

In the midst of adversity,
When the forces of the enemy are raging,
You must prepare to fight; get ready for war.

You must release those cares;
Release all the worries unto Me; the True Warrior.
No longer will you fret over the evildoers.
No longer will you carry the stress and strain.

From this day forward, fight the good fight.
Seek Me earnestly through prayer;
Through My word.

Let's Take a Stand

So many struggles; too may wars to fight.
Constantly battling; why not do what's right?
Being ridiculed just for taking a stand.
Working and supporting to bring forth the vision.

What happened to the integrity?
Where's the true love for ministry?
Where's the zeal, the unity, the thoughtfulness?

He sees and knows all things;
He's looking down on us even now.
Let's walk in the divine order of God.
Let's walk into the place where we're called to be.

At the Breaking of Day

Stand firm on My promises;
Stand firm on your faith.
Believing that you will receive
Your breakthrough; your miracle to come.

Stand firm in the midst of your circumstances
Knowing that these things come to perfect you;
To instill in you the things of My Father;
The things that will propel you closer to Him.

Seek Him the more;
It's not as long as it has been.
Your morning is suddenly upon you.
Rejoice!

Will You Say Yes?

You say that you love Me,
But yet you defy Me;
You do things contrary to My word.

You say you're with Me,
But your actions say that you're against Me.
Why is it so hard to do what's right?
Why do you find it difficult
To follow simple commands?
Why stifle the vision, when you can help
Bring it to fruition?

What I ask for is not much.
Simply submit your will to Mine.
Just put your hands in Mine,
And trust Me with your life.
Just say yes.

One in Him

So much is going on in the ministry now.
Frustrations, confusion.
Not much togetherness; not a lot of unity;
Very little love.

Why bother coming if you're not going to
Support the calling; the vision that's given to
The angel of the house?

Don't they understand that when they fight him,
They're fighting God?
When they curse him, they're cursing God?
Do they even realize that when they hurt him,
They're hurting God?

When will there be peace?
When will we all learn to love one another
As the bible says we should?
When will we come to understand that there are no
Separate entities in ministry?
We are all members of the same body.
We are one!

He's With You

Circumstances come to test your faith.
Buy My word says, "I'll never leave you,
Nor forsake you."
God is with you; even when you're in the
Midst of the fire.
God is with you.

He sees and knows of everything that
You go through.
God will be there to encourage you,
And tell you that you're going to make it.

The Love of the Savior

No greater love than the love
The Savior has, that He would
Lay down His life for a friend.

How awesome is the Lord,
To minister to His people.
To reach them at their weakest point,
And bring them to a place of blessing.
A place of restoration and healing.

How awesome, and how excellent is the Lord, God of Host.
The Holy One of Israel.
The provider of all that I need.
The sustainer of life.
Jesus, the precious one of Zion.
My Savior, and my friend.

Rest in My peace.
Rest in My joy, hope and love.
Always remember you can hide
Under the shelter of My wings.

Come to my Rescue

Make haste to see about me.
I'm calling on Your holy and righteous name.
In my distress, I cry out to You.
O God, help me in my troubled times.

I long to feel Your peace;
Grace and mercy sustained.
Be thou, my protection;
My strong tower and shield.

Close to You

Let me have an experience with You
That transcends any other.
God, just to be in Your presence means
More than anything to me.

Being consumed by Your anointing;
Just to hear Your voice,
That sweet, still voice, oh Lord, is
What calms all of my fears, and removes every doubt.

Thank You for being my everything, Father.
You're my counselor, my provider, my healer, and ruler;
The center of my joy.
Jesus, You're my very best friend.

Wonderful is He

Such a wonderful Savior You are.
So kind, so glorious.
So wondrous, and true.
Always forgiving, always providing,
Always giving unto me
From Your riches.

What a privilege it is to
Be in Your presence.
Just to feel You near me,
Gives me the assurance that I can stand any storm
I can go through any battle.
I can handle the pressure because You,
Oh God, are there with me.

With You, I Can Make It

In life, many circumstances come.
Struggles, trials and tests;
Many things we're faced with.

But because of You, God, we know that
We can overcome them all.
When life seems hopeless, You give us hope.
When it seems impossible, You, my God, make it possible.

With You, it is possible to stand.
With You, it's possible to stand firm on
Every promise You've made.

I stand here now, confident and at
Peace because You are with me.
I'm stronger in faith.

Seek My Face

Come now, My children.
Come before Me with your
Hearts full of praise.
Come, lay your petitions before Me.
Pour out of your heart in My presence.

Too many burdens for you to carry;
Yes, too many cares.
Lay them all before Me, my sons; my daughters.
Lay down every stress and strain.

You must seek Me earnestly,
While I may be found.
Walk in the authority that I have placed in you.
Stand firm upon My word.

Dwell with Him

Search me and try me;
Make me an instrument of praise.
One fit for service in Your kingdom.

Try my heart
See my soul
Lord, make me fit for worship;
For service in Your kingdom.

Come inside and dwell
Come inside, and sup with me,
As I sup with You.

Dwell inside this temple
Fill it with more of You;
More of Your spirit and power;
More of Your love and grace.

Why Compromise?

Time and time again, I ask myself,
Why? Why did you do what you did?
What was the purpose of it all?
What good did it really do?

Nearly lost sight of my destiny;
The ultimate reason for my existence.
Risked losing it all;
My place in You; my joy, my peace;
True happiness—only to be given by You.
All for something that would never be.

My place in You is far too precious.
My self-worth is far too valuable.
It all means far too much to be
Taken lightly; to be thrown away.
My heart's desire is to please You;
To be a yielded vessel.

So as I come before You now
In total reverence and humility
Laying before You; seeking Your face.
I open my heart to You,
Releasing unto You every care
Every struggle, every battle.

Release now unto me,
More of Your grace and love,
More of Your strength and power,
More of Your anointing.

Stand the Storm

Struggle after struggle;
Trial after trial.
What are You preparing me for?
Show me what it is You want me to see.
Make me the kind of woman
You want me to be.

"My child, You have been fearfully,
And wonderfully made.
Your steps have been ordered by My hand.
You've been created for greatness
You are destined for good things.

Each trial brings new strength.
Every test brings more wisdom.
Stand firm on your faith."

My Prayer

Bless my life, dear God.
See all of my works;
See that my heart's committed to service.
See my desire to build Your kingdom.
Strengthen my walk with You; refresh and renew me now.
Refine my heart for ministry.
Anoint me now with fresh oil.

There's no other way I know than that of ministry.
So, keep my feet planted, I ask dear Lord.
Grounded and rooted on a sure foundation.

There's no other way to live
Than to be in right relationship with You, Father.
The one true Savior and Redeemer.

To Be Like Him

My desire is to be a light to those who live in darkness.
A follower of Your Son, Jesus Christ.
A true instrument of praise.

There's so much confusion; so much deception in the body.
Some wonder, who's really true at heart?
Who is a genuine follower of Christ?
Who are they really living for?

In these days and times,
It's important to stand up for what is right;
We must live holy before our God.
We must long to be like Him.

You Keep on Blessing Me

There's no way I can live without You.
For You are so mighty, and so powerful,
Yet gentle and full of compassion.

You see my needs, and supply them all.
In times of weakness,
You're there to catch me when I fall.
You just keep on blessing me.

When the trials of life get the best of me,
There's always a word from Your throne.
It lifts me, and fills my heart with hope.
You just keep on blessing me.

www.ingramcontent.com/pod-product-compliance
Lightning Source LLC
Chambersburg PA
CBHW070950040426

42443CB00012B/3293